MANAGING
UPWARDS

THE BEGINNER'S GUIDE IN
MANAGING YOUR BOSS

I.K. BUTCHER

KENOSIS BOOKS: BE THE BEST YOU – SELF-IMPROVEMENT SERIES

SUBSCRIBE AND GET YOUR FREE eBOOK!

If you want to improve the quality of your attention and are willing to do other means to improve your focus and concentration, then this book will definitely help you in that. This book contains the ff:

1. Top Foods to increase your Focus and Concentration

2. Foods you can intake daily to improve your focus

3. Best Juices to Improve your focus

4. Healthy Habits and Eating Style to Improve Focus

..... and much more!

So take action, and scan the QR CODE and/or <u>Subscribe</u> *to our* **Kenosis Books - Be The Best You: Self-Improvement Series** *mailing list and be updated in our latest books and promotions!*

MANAGING UPWARDS

THE BEGINNER'S GUIDE IN MANAGING YOUR BOSS

TO MY WIFE AND MY SON, THIS BOOK IS FOR YOU.

Table of Contents

CHAPTER 1

INTRODUCTION

Management ideas over the years have bordered around subordinates, products, resources and projects. This leaves out the all-important concept of managing your relationship with your superior(s).

The boss-subordinate relationship is like a see-saw where the parties on either end depend on each other and finding an equilibrium is key. This book is aimed at helping you establish and maintain a healthy relationship with your boss.

The core of the book is outlined in 3 major moves, the fourth being our checkmate move that will guide you all the way through your journey of managing your boss as a strategy of work place excellence.

At the end of each of the chapters explaining the moves, there is/are points of action that will help you swing into action and be rewarded with immediate results. I advise to take a move per week so that you have enough time to study and practice the strategies you are about to learn.

You will find some immediate results and others over time. Whatever the case, get a pen, take some notes, let's win it.

THE WHY OF MANAGING YOUR BOSS

Imagine working for a company where you report directly to just one person, your immediate boss. You have worked very hard over the years building great relationships with your colleagues and juniors, you have hit targets, gotten promoted a couple of times and are well known as an achiever within the company, then you have a new employee transferred to the department you head.

This employee has a good track record and seems to have excellent skills but he doesn't communicate, he's assuming and takes decisions you have not authorized. His attitude begins to affect you and the results of the team you supervise.

Do you think that is a good employee? Can you work with that? What will be your response in such situation?

Now, imagine this is how your boss views you even though you are doing your best. It is obvious this imbalance between the subordinate and the boss is a recipe for disaster. Now, you can begin to imagine different scenarios in your workplace and how synergy and a cordial relationship with your boss can make or ruin your effectiveness in the workplace.

A lack of understanding between you and your boss puts you in a bad stance at least relative to him/her, will hinder proper planning and can cost you a lot because the blame will most likely fall on you when things go awry and begin to affect the health of your company.

You must see the company as an organism. Your department is an organ with your boss as principal control. If you are not doing well with your boss, the organ is sick and inevitably the organism cannot function properly.

Your inability to maintain a cordial relationship with your boss puts a lot of stress on your colleagues and other organs of the company. This is not where you want to be found. Not in the problematic organ lest you be ejected from the system.

Of course, some bosses can be difficult and be the problem themselves, but this is where your adaptability and managing upward skills become most useful. You must succeed no matter the conditions.

BENEFITS OF MANAGING YOUR BOSS

Managing your boss may seem a bit unfamiliar a topic but it is crucial to your success in the work place and it is as simple as having a good relationship that may even benefit you outside the work environment. Let's take a quick view of some of those benefits to expect from this adventure

1. **Health:** work can often come with various levels of stress whether perceived or actual. Your boss and your relationship with him has a big influence on how much stress you have to

go through at the end of the day. A great work place relationship with your boss and good communication will reduce the amount of stress and pressure you have to endure making work somewhat more exciting. This will in turn ensure that you are mentally and physically healthy.

2. **Motivation**: an exciting work life and reduced mental strain comes with boosts in your levels of motivation. The good feeling that comes with knowing your boss is supportive and working well with you will make you work harder and much more efficiently knowing your efforts will be appreciated.

3. **Development**: alongside with a healthy relationship with your boss comes constructive criticisms, good feedback and a wealth of experience to glean from. A cordial relationship with your boss will foster great communication in which your boss is able to show you much more effective ways to get things done and regularly gives you details of your performance and how to improve.

4. **Advancement**: everyone wants to scale up. The key to your promotions and recommendations for opportunities of greater benefits within or outside your workplace lies in the hands of your boss. Learn to please him/her, have great interactions with them and watch doors open for you.

Are you ready to take responsibility and make the difference? Are you ready to ensure that your boss sees you as vital rather than a bane? Let's get started.

CHAPTER 2

MOVE 1: UNDERSTANDING YOURSELF

Hopefully you have read and taken time to muse over the contents of the introduction. If you have done that, by now you know how important relationships are – particularly the relationship you're in with your boss.

Identifying and understanding yourself is the first thing to do if you must build great relationships anywhere. Who are you in this place? What are your responsibilities? What do you want? What are your goals? These are some of the questions you will need to answer and that this section seeks to help you highlight.

Knowing yourself and understanding your personal goals will help you decipher who is important to you, what is most important and how to handle the situations you will be forced to face in the work place. More importantly is, it will allow you to present yourself the way you want your boss to see you, helping him/her discover how best to work with you.

WHO AM I, WHAT DO I STAND FOR?
This is the first thing you need to find out. Who really are you?

The human mind is such that each individual has a particular pattern of thought based on experiences, temperament and a whole lot of other factors. Being able to identify how you think and what influences your decisions gives you an idea of where you need to work on to achieve workplace excellence.

The most important thing for you in the workplace is to answer the question of purpose. The Japanese have a model of self-discovery called Ikigai which we'll use as a guide here in discovering purpose.

It is based on answering the four fundamental questions of life;

1. Passion as in what do you love doing?

2. Vocation as in what are you actually good at doing?
3. Profession as in what can you do that people will be willing to pay you for?
4. Mission as in what the world needs?

While answering these questions ultimately stands in a broader sense to actualize a fulfilled and happy life, we can narrow them down a bit and adapt them to a guide for fulfilment in the workplace.

QUESTION 1: WHAT ARE THE THINGS YOU LOVE DOING?

Your answers should border around your hobbies, positive habits, and things you enjoy doing.

- Do you like puzzles?
- Do you like to read?
- Do you like to create?
- Do you enjoy music?

Whatever you enjoy doing that doesn't feel like work to you, those are the answers to this question. While this may seem unrelated, they may be your escape route or source of inspiration when the going gets tough at work. Highlighting them will also help you engage in them more often and perhaps identify portions of your work that they can influence.

For example, if music helps you relax, you can employ music when you are under a lot of pressure at work. It will lift your energy levels and prevent unpleasant emotional responses. Just ensure this doesn't get in the way of your job and only do things that your kind of work permit.

If you are the type that does well with puzzles and trying to put pieces of information together, you can bring this ability to use at work in the case that your boss is not very open with information or does not communicate well enough. Instead of pressing them to the point of irritation, just bring on your "A-GAME" of puzzle solving in the task at hand and everything will be ok.

Whatever it is you like, find elements of it in your job and that will make you enjoy your job even more. It is a known fact that when you enjoy what you are doing, you will seemingly have less troubles getting along with everyone you have to work with. Get the positive energy from your passions and you will have an unending source of that level of energy at work.

QUESTION 2: WHAT ARE YOU ACTUALLY GOOD AT DOING?

This describes your skills not mere hobbies now.

- Are you a good listener?
- Are you a good orator?
- Are you good at writing?
- Do you have good presentation skills?

In the workplace these are the things you want to know. You should be able to list out all the things you are able to do almost effortlessly. Some of them may be natural abilities, others, things you need to learn. Know what you can do and what you cannot. The more things you can do, the more versatile you are, the more valuable you are at work especially to your boss.

QUESTION 3: WHAT CAN YOU CAN DO THAT YOU CAN BE REWARDED FOR?

This is where you really align to work. Of all the skills and abilities that you have, how many are actually valuable in your job. For example, if you are working as a customer service agent, you should possess the following skills amongst others.

- Good listening abilities
- Assertiveness
- Good communication
- Multi-tasking abilities

The onus lies on you to ensure that you possess all or at least most of the skills that your job requires, to continuously exercise and develop them so that you do not become a liability to your boss and colleagues.

Particularly, you should mark out those skills that are critical to your job and can give you an edge over other employees. These are skills that will make the job easier for your boss as you are more efficient.

This will inevitably put you in the good records of your boss and help you foster a great boss-employee relationship. No matter how much your boss likes you, if you are not hitting the targets and showing efficiency at work, you are sure to have loads of problems with that sort of boss.

QUESTION 4: WHAT DOES THE WORLD NEED?

You might be wondering how the need of the world affects you and your boss. Every company is established to meet a need. When the needs of people are met, they pay. In the actual sense, the question of the need of the world has been answered for you by the company you work for and it influences what they highlight as their mission statement.

From their mission the company dishes out responsibilities, targets and objectives to everyone. You must identify what your general responsibilities are and much more the targets you must achieve within set periods of time.

When you are able to answer the above four questions, the next thing is to write them down, think thoroughly through them and find a synergy among your answers. The result is an effortless drive towards success. For the Japanese, the Ikigai is a meditative process used to actualize a happy life, so if we have adapted it for workplace excellence you should not neglect the meditative aspects.

This is a reflection you should have regularly to keep your focus and re-evaluate yourself.

OTHER QUESTIONS

1. **What are your goals**: it is not enough to just keep trying to meet targets set for you by your boss and company. You should have personal goals in the workplace. Makes you accountable and helps you track your development as a person. Below are four simple steps to help you set personal development goals in the workplace
   a. Have a vision: where do you see yourself in the nearest future? You should be able to put down in black and white what your desires for work are. For example, if you are a salesman your vision could be making $50,000 worth of sales in excess of the company target per month. You know what is realistic, you know your current performance, now push the bar a bit higher.

b. Pen down a plan: spelling out feasible steps will ensure you are in line with your vision for yourself. If you are that salesman, you can plan to
   - Double your customer base
   - Reach out to old customers that you lost contact with
   - Encourage existing customers to buy more
c. Make routine checks: this is simply tracking your progress. Make notes, use metrics to see how far you have done against your goal. You should have a record that makes your progress measurable and allows you to see where you stand in relation to the target.
d. Update your plans: this is a very important step. Circumstances change, even your desires as a person are subject to change. You have to use a planning method that accommodates these changes. Have new plans, set new goals and keep going. The idea is that you constantly have new things to work towards. This would eventually boost your productivity.

2. **Do you love autonomy**: this can be a peculiar challenge for some people. While everyone deserves some levels of autonomy for effectiveness, you actually cannot work all by yourself. You will need the guide and support of others especially your boss. If you always want to call the shots and make the decisions of how and when, you will run into problems especially if your boss has a similar trait. You have to notice this about yourself and know when to push the brakes. Give your boss the opportunity to guide you and run things the way you want while owning your space. A good way to do this is to prove your worth and be trustworthy. If your boss can trust you, he will most likely delegate things to you and give you a free-hand to handle many things without his present monitoring. It is really all in the mind, if you present yourself as efficient and trustworthy, you will be treated as such but if you do not seem to have much to offer nobody will trust you to work on your own.

3. **How emotionally stable are you**: emotions can be a bane to you if not properly managed. You cannot allow emotions from your ordeals outside work to affect your relationships and efficiency at work. This can be really difficult since humans are emotional beings but you must check it. If you are not a very emotionally stable person then that is a place you have to work on and be constantly aware of. Don't get too excited about success so you don't lose focus and don't allow offenses get the best of you. Your boss will offend and that is certain, this could be in his/her manner of speech or even an error of judgement but you must find a way of expressing your grievance without creating a scene or putting a negatively indelible mark on your relationship with him/her.

SKILL IS VALUE, EXPERIENCE IS VALUE

We have gone through highlighting your skills and abilities. You will learn more of these on the job and get better in each of these skills. The pace of this learning and development process is however a function of how deliberate you are. You have to consciously learn new skills and sharpen those that you already have.

The brain is a network of neurons with definite pathways for each process that it controls including sleep, playing an instrument, typing, listening and any action you can think of. Scientifically, it is said that the more you practice an action, the more neurons your brain dedicates to carrying out that action. This means faster, easier and more efficient work is done when you practice.

It is not enough to learn a new skill, you have to consciously put it to work on the job and even off work sometimes just to ensure that you are getting better all the time.

POINTS OF ACTION

- Take a walk and meditate on the things you enjoy doing
- Research the Ikigai and practice it in your personal life

- Make a list of goals you plan to achieve in the next month and write a detailed plan on how to achieve them

CHAPTER 3

MOVE 2: UNDERSTANDING THE BOSS

This is the second big move in managing your boss. Many managers actually do this to some extent but what sets you apart from the rest is the conscious effort and the extent to which to know your boss and pay attention to his/her needs.

Knowing your boss doesn't actually imply intruding in his/her personal life to set the record straight, it involves knowing why and how he/she does things at work. For example, what drives him/her to work, does he/she communicate effectively, how he/she responds to workplace challenges and so on.

A few of the most important things to check are highlighted below but you should observe as much as possible and put into consideration your observations when as you deal with your boss on a day to day basis.

WHAT KIND OF PERSON IS YOUR BOSS?

This describes the kind of approach your boss has to work and his/her work relationships. You will want to find out if he/she is a jovial and laid back kind of boss that allows his staff to work at their own pace and with their own style or if he likes to be in control of every detail.

Based on their approach to work the kind boss you have maybe

1. **The disorganised**: these kinds of bosses are often all over the place, very active and actually get more done than you can imagine. They just don't have an order to things neither are they often informed of their schedule until the meeting is already starting. The best way to handle this kind of boss is to bring order to him without being the antagonist. It just means sending him enough reminders and anticipating what is the next important move.
2. **The organised**: they are often marked by a good-looking appearance and a structured way of doing things. If you are

going to get along well with them, don't go late to meetings and always make sure you are tidy. The moment they sense that you are not organised, they will stop seeing you as efficient or trustworthy.

3. **The detail freak**: they want to know the nitty gritty of everything. When, how, why and who are the things you want to know and report to them as often as possible if you must satisfy them. This will make them trust you.

4. **The result focused**: they are only concerned with what, as in what needs to be done and what has been done. They set out the objectives and await the results, how the result is achieved is not much of their concern. Working well with such a boss means to spare them tiny details, just give them a report of the achievements so far and the next line of action that you think is most ideal and that will be it.

5. **The interactive**: this kind of boss wants your feedback, involves you in decision making and wants to work with you all the way. Their strength is effective communication. They may not press you so much for details but they require a back and forth of important information.

6. **The non-interactive**: this kind of boss is the exact opposite of the interactive boss. They only talk to you when they have information that they think is okay for you to know. The best way to work with such a boss is to simply follow directives and only asked questions about what you really need to know while giving solid reasons why that information is important.

WHAT DRIVES YOUR BOSS?

The source of motivation of your boss is important to you. What most bosses require from you apart from fitting into your job description is your cooperation and support. Knowing his source of motivation even puts you a step ahead since you can help to create the enabling environment that your boss needs to work effectively.

The fact that you are a part of what makes things work for him, makes you important to him and distinguishes you amongst others. You may want to find out how your boss works best for example,

- An orderly environment
- A competitive atmosphere
- A sense of control
- Positive attitudes
- An enthusiastic environment

Whatever it is that allows your boss enjoy his work should be something that comes from you or that you an active part of.

WHAT TURNS HIM/HER OFF?

Now you know what motivates your boss. It is also very important to know what drives his energy levels down, does he get worked up when the place is noisy and does he easily irritated by a lack of definite information? Whatever it is that makes your boss less productive is worth noting and avoiding.

A list of other things that may be of negative influence may include:

- Time pressure
- Unnecessary details
- A lack of effective communication
- Conflict
- Disorder
- Negative Surprises

WHAT ARE HIS/HER STRENGTHS AND WEAKNESSES?

It is very easy to associate the boss just with the tag "BOSS" rather than as flesh and blood prone to errors and having areas of strength and weaknesses. Identifying the strengths of your boss will help you see things you can emulate and things you can relax about since he/she already has it covered.

On the other hand, knowing where your boss is not so strong allows you to identify ways of being of good support to him/her. This should in no way breed unnecessary familiarity that will inspire disrespect. The most important thing is that you can give adequate support and you can learn effectively the things that are worthy of emulation.

To help you identify these areas of strength and weakness, here are a couple of questions you may need to answer:

1. How does your boss handle pressure?
2. Is he/she prone to emotional outbursts?
3. How do your colleagues and other co-workers view your boss?
4. What does everyone like about him/her?
5. What does everyone complain of about him/her?
6. Are you currently giving your best effort under your boss? Why or why not?
7. What can your boss do to get even more dedication and support from you?

HOW DOES YOUR BOSS COMMUNICATE?

You must know how to get important information from your boss and how to pass them to him. Does your boss prefer formal writing or does he refer a phone call? Does he prefer to be briefed before a physical official meeting or can you just jump into a meeting with him?

These are things you need to observe and utilize so you can build rapport with your boss. Something very important to note is how well they communicate. If your boss communicates well then all you need is to be attentive and ask questions where need be.

In the case that your boss is not very good at expressing things in clear terms, you have some work to do. You can either continue to ask questions to clarify things until you are certain what it is they want or are trying to pass across or you could put forward what you understand from their briefing.

If your understanding of what they said is incorrect, sending it to them puts the responsibility on them to further clarify things. Again, it all depends on your kind of boss on what strategy you need to employ.

RESPECT IS MUTUAL, HUMILITY IS SERVICE

Getting to know your boss give you a lot of information about his/her personality. You will see his/her strengths and naturally respect him/her for that. This kind of respect is natural and mutual as humans we are naturally predisposed to respecting and honouring good traits that we find in others.

However, you will also find out the weaknesses of your boss. It is very possible that you even have the strengths that he/she lacks and have to cover up for the lapses. This is where humility and true character steps in. If you fail to duly respect and honour your boss despite his/her shortcomings, then you lack humility and character and surely things cannot work well between you and such a boss.

Humility is your service in continuous support for your boss. This is something you have to take note of and constantly work on. In your service, your loyalty will be tested and if you pass, you have gotten yourself a favourite spot with your boss. Every boss likes a supportive and loyal person that they know they can always rely on.

POINTS OF ACTION

- Highlight ten (10) strengths and weaknesses of your boss
- How do you plan to compensate for his weaknesses

Chapter 4

MOVE 3: UNDERSTANDING THE COMPANY

Understanding your boss is a milestone completed, now you need to cross another hurdle that will help both yourself and your boss, which is, understanding the company. Having a full grasp of the vision of the company you work for and where they stand in relation to that vision will help you know the extent of pressure that your boss is handling and how to help.

Understanding the company will involve knowing the current strategies, the internal politics and game players in it. It boils down to how well you are able to get information, and use it in strategic ways, from your boss, colleagues, and your portfolio relationships. It is also important to understand the culture, norms, and values in your company. What are acceptable practices? What are not acceptable?

Having this edge will help you see the perspectives of your boss, and the leadership further on top of him/her.

UNDERSTANDING YOUR COMPANY THROUGH YOUR BOSS:

There are two ways you can go about this. You can either build personal rapport with the boss or build professional rapport. The way you go depends on both the personality of your boss and which is an easier path for you to follow.

Whatever the path you choose, the aim is for you to know what decisions are being made and what are the major events occurring that will affect the overall health of the company. It will also help you understand clearly what the strategic goals of the company which the boss would have just declared to the team as objectives. Now you know not just the goals but the reason behind this set objectives and what your boss's take on the situation is.

UNDERSTANDING THE COMPANY THROUGH YOUR COLLEAGUES

Information is power in the workplace, the more you know the better your stance. This is not to say you should go around sniffing for information, but you should have good working and personal relationships with your colleagues on the same team and in other departments so much so that no vital information eludes you.

In this strategy, information flows to you from different sources and you can make good use of these in helping your boss better via suggestions and instinctive actions on the job. You just have to be popular. Be known for who you are in your department and beyond and people will naturally be drawn to you. You then know what is happening in other department and how you can make sure that your department is not lagging behind in its contributions to the overall success of the company.

Once your boss knows that your ideas in the team (which will spring from careful analysis of all the information you have received) helps to put the department at par and drives success in line with the direction of the company, you gain credibility. The respect is there, and everyone wants to hear what you have to say.

UNDERSTANDING THE COMPANY VIA PORTFOLIO RELATIONSHIPS

Portfolio relationships are those that you have with seniors in other departments. These could be people who are colleagues of your boss or even superior to him. Often your quality of work and popularity amongst the members of staff will earn you these kinds of relationships. They would often be able to provide you with vital insider information from even executive levels in some instances.

You should wisely make this kind of access that you have known to your boss. It will make him respect you more and consolidate whatever interactions you have had with him her. The best kinds of information come from these relationships because they are genuine, strategic to the company, and give you an edge above others who do not have the kind of access that you have. Another advantage to this is that it opens you up to opportunities that will advance your career.

Having created these relationships, you will have all the information that you need about the company, know how they affect your boss and work and can then make strategic decisions.

STRATEGIC THINKING

This should be another long theory or load of information. But it is better you form this yourself so it becomes practical and applicable in your present scenario. Now you have the relationships and the strategic information, how do you use it? The answers to this is in your ability to think strategically and make plans and solid moves. To help you, you should ask the following questions and then make all the necessary plans in your favour:

1. What are the trends outside and inside the company?
2. What can you anticipate about these trends?
3. How much does this information affect the company?
4. How does it affect my direct boss?
5. How will it affect me and my ability to work?
6. Will this put more pressure on my boss?
7. What must I do to make the best of the current situation?
8. What major contributions of mine will make the job easier for the team and my boss?
9. Are there people I can work with to utilize this information to maximize profit for me, my boss, and the department?

By the time you answer these questions and a few others that will pop up as you think through them, you should be able to come up with the perfect plan for efficiency and effectivity. This is strategic thinking.

POINTS OF ACTION

- Analyse the kinds of people you know?
- What kinds of information get to you, are they strategic or mere gossip?

- Using the information in this chapter, make plans on getting and using vital company information.
- Think about how to use this information to come up with best approach that your boss will appreciate.

CHAPTER 5

MOVE 4: CHECKMATE- FINDING AN EQUILIBRIUM

We have taken quite a while identifying you and what works for you and sometime highlighting important things to know about your boss and the company. The **checkmate move** is to build a bridge among these identities in a bid to work together effectively to achieve common goal. Unlike chess, this checkmate move is not about defeating but sustaining a balance.

Such an equilibrium as you are trying to build at this point is marked by a unity of expectations and its adaptability to suite the work styles and needs of both parties. In the checkmate move, your goal is to start and maintain a relationship based on:

1. **Trust**: every boss wants to work with someone they can trust. They have targets set for them, pressures from their superiors and personal goals and cannot afford a team member that will hinder their progress in any way.
   To foster trust you will need to be
   a. Consistent: when there is a regular pattern to how you work, it makes your work predictable to your boss and they can easily and accurately plan with that information. Often times, an inconsistent employee is not reliable and that is not something a boss will fancy in his employee. It is better to be consistently disorganized than to be organized today and disorganized tomorrow. You will be most likely confusing your boss as to who you are.
   b. Honest: you cannot afford to underplay issues or try to cover up facts. Let your boss always know the true situation of things so that problems can be well tackles and future mishaps can be prevented. When your boss cannot take the information you supply without having to double check it makes working with you difficult.

The importance of trust is seen in that it aids easy delegation and a sense of dependability one on another all the course of work.

2. Free flow of information: this is one of the most important factors in any relationship at all. Have you ever lost touch with a person for a while? Do you observe how difficult kick-starting the talking is when you finally meet? This is exactly what it is like when there is a break in communication between boss and employee. Not only is kickstarting the process more difficult, there will always be times of misunderstandings. You cannot assume that you know what your boss wants. Always try to establish channels of communication that always suits your boss and keep that channel open.

3. Good use of time and resources: you must realize that time is money and resources are scarce. That is obvious really but many seem to lose sight of these facts. You cannot afford to spend the limited time your boss has on trivial matters or mismanage the resources they have made available to you. Always seeks ways to maximize the time they spend with you in getting clarifications and producing quality results from the resources they avail you.

HOW TO SAY NO AND PROVIDE A BETTER SUGGESTION

The one and important skill you need here is "assertiveness." Being assertive simply means being able to say no or reject an opinion without the feeling of guilt or aggressiveness. Assertiveness is a skill that comes to play for many people only occasionally as a matter of chance rather than a choice they are in charge of. There are 5 steps to assertiveness that you will need to practice to sharpen this ability to say "no"

1. **Kill the guilt:** almost oddly, there is a sense of guilt that seem to overwhelm us when we have to say no. This feeling accounts for the inability of many people to say no to a

suggestion leading them to take more work than normal. If you don't remind yourself that you actually have the right to say "no" you will end up under more stress than you can handle and feel frustrated. This is the first thing you must convince yourself of; "I have the right to say no, to negate opinions that I don't agree with and to reject responsibilities that are not mine."

2. **Have a solid reason**: it will help both you and your boss to have a good reason for your action. This explanation should be brief and is absolutely not compulsory. It only helps to portray you as co-operative while you're airing your views. Always begin with the principle, as principles are timeless foundations of reason that are difficult to negate.

3. **Offer any helpful suggestion:** the reason for feeling guilty when you say no is probably that you feel you have let your boss down or you will be disappointing them. Being able to offer an alternative might help you feel helpful even though you are not doing their bidding and convince your boss and/or colleagues of your reasonable stance. In fact, if you apply some creativity, you can come up with a much better suggestion that your boss will appreciate.

Keep in mind as well that there are even types of bosses who do not like "Yes" Men or Women. To them, they don't add any value nor give another perspective. They will just accept whatever the boss will say. This new generation of bosses truly appreciate the fact that if they will rely on their own perspective, it may be detrimental to the department or to the company, in the long run. Hence, those employees who can say no to them will gain their trust as these people are willing to contradict their boss for the best interest of the company or department.

4. **Maintain your position:** no matter how much you try to convince some people that you cannot help them at the moment, or that you have another perspective, they keep on coming with the same request or insisting on their view. They

just want to dump the pressure on you. This is where you must stand your ground. Repeat your stance and your reasons again and again in different ways until they get your point. This step is very important if you have been the utterly submissive type in the past. It difficult for people to accept that you are saying "no" for the first time and they will try to pressure you into being like that again. Continue to be assertive and drive your point sincerely and clearly.

Saying "no" to unnecessary requests, demands you cannot meet up with or opinions you do not agree with is only one part of the whole picture. Assertiveness is an attitude of respect, honesty, and conviction. If you don't have an honest reason for what you do and how, you cannot be convinced, you will only be making excuses. Even when you are honest and convinced, when you are known to not respect others and their opinions and are always trying to impose your views without regards for the viability of others, no one will listen you neither will they esteem your opinions.

Remember, it is only a checkmate when you create a balance between you and your boss. Now check the correlations and adjust.

Always keep in mind that when you become assertive of your position, there is also a possibility that the other side has perspective that you don't understand. In those cases, be open, pay attention, and listen. We don't know that it can be a start of a good dialogue and be the trigger of better, more creative ideas or alternatives.

POINTS OF ACTION

- Make a comparison of yours and your boss' traits and highlight changes you have to make to asset to him/her
- Make a written statement of commitment and honesty to your boss as it concerns your job. What and how will you do to his/her that will ensure this sort of openness and commitment?

CONCLUSION

NEVER FORGET

Workplace excellence is a discipline that requires continuous and intentional effort. If managing your boss effectively is one of the strategies you have chosen to employ, as you should, you must realise that it is also an ongoing process of learning, adjusting, and acting in such a way that your boss values his work relationship with you and can allude to your outstanding work ethics.

Never forget the points of action in this book, visit them regularly. Never forget the checkmate move it is the crux of the matter, the equilibrium of respect and trust you need to have a great time working for your boss.

BONUS

THE SOFT SIDE: HOW TO WIN YOUR BOSS BY BUILDING A FRIENDLY RELATIONSHIP

Not all bosses are the typical textbook type boss – like the hard, strict, and distant and that they maintain a wide gap between work and personal life. Some of the bosses, remove that gap and treats you like a friend and even family.

These bosses, for example, invite their teams to their house so you can meet their family. These bosses are very much open to talk about the activities of their families, talk about their children, and share experiences as well. These bosses believe that the key to building teams is to build personal relationships by building genuine friendships on top of the work.

Here are top three recommendations to do for these kinds of bosses.

1. Know their family – this will let your boss know how much you care as well for their wellbeing
   a. Get to know their spouses, their children, the rest of their family when possible
   b. Know their likes and dislikes
   c. Common interests
   d. Any similarities with your family
2. Remember important dates – a short greeting at the right time will mean a lot to the bosses
   a. Birthdays
   b. Anniversaries
   c. Father's Day/Mother's Day
   d. Holidays where you can give special greetings
3. Go for the extra mile – this is a timeless principle. Those who can do more, will be given more.
   a. At work – doing more than what is expected of you
   b. Personally – offering friendly help when needed

c. Treats – sharing some snacks food while at work
d. Gatherings – accepting invitations for team gatherings and celebrations
e. Souvenirs – sharing some tokens back to your boss and colleagues when you travel

Hence, the last portion in going the extra mile is universal but adaptation to local culture / company culture may vary. Some practices may be acceptable in one country but are not acceptable in another. Thus, careful consideration, is needed before attempting to act on such recommendations.

Moreover, doing more than what is expected at work is what separates achievers from those who are already happy with their current tasks and responsibilities.

If you are desiring more upward mobility in the organization, this will definitely provide great help to you. Some of the bosses will even discourage you and highlight the spirit of work-life balance. However, if you think about it work-life balance presumes that there is no "life" at work. This presumption does not apply to the bosses who remove the gap between life and work. To them, there is just life and part of its network of meanings are their families, their friends, and their colleagues!

REFERENCES AND CITATIONS

- Gabarro, J. J., & Kotter, J. P. (2008). *Managing Your Boss (Harvard Business Review Classics)*. Harvard Business Review Press.

- Jay, R. (2002). *How to Manage Your Boss: Developing the Perfect Working Relationship* (1st ed.). Ft Pr.

OTHER PROMOTED BOOKS

M. L. PILGRIM

SCAN ME

SUBSCRIBE AND GET YOUR FREE eBOOK!

If you are looking for investment that offers you inflationary protection and that reduces your investment risk significantly, precious metals such as gold, silver, and platinum (amongst others) is the way to go. Unlike paper money, precious metals have a finite supply and you cannot print more of them, and because of this, precious metals offer authentic insurance against political and financial upheavals. This book will share about the ff:

WHAT ARE PRECIOUS METALS?
WHY YOU SHOULD INVEST? - THE UPSIDE AND DOWNSIDE
WHO SHOULD INVEST?
WHAT PRECIOUS METALS SHOULD YOU INVEST IN?
WAYS TO INVEST IN PRECIOUS METALS
CONCLUSION- WHEN SHOULD YOU INVEST?

The primary aim of this eBook is to open young investors' eyes to the infinite possibilities of investment in precious metals. This eBook shows you that you have the time advantage of youth and the ability to take on more risks, and that these advantages can help you make better and bigger investment profits, whether you choose to invest in gold, palladium, copper, silver, or platinum and whether you choose to invest in coins, bars, rounds, or precious metal ETFs.

So take action, and scan the QR CODE and/or Subscribe to our newsletter for more updates!

ABOUT THE AUTHOR

M. L. Pilgrim lost millions when he was starting as an entrepreneur but only his consistent belief in the power of the subconscious mind has brought him to his success. He is very active investing with majority of his portfolio in precious metals and stocks. Also, he invests in bonds, mutual funds, UITFs, and in other businesses in real estate, power generation, banking, logistics, retail, and telecommunications.

He worked across 10 countries always fascinated with the beauty of nature, culture, and traditions. He is a versatile author writing both fiction and non-fiction. He is a traveler, a dedicated father, a loving son, and a responsible brother.

He strongly believes that everyone can succeed both in business, relationships, society, and other aspects if they only have the right information and knowledge on how to use that information properly.

M. L. Pilgrim uses a pen name as he doesn't want to show himself as a definitive expert. Instead, he is in this journey with his readers like a "pilgrim" and wants to travel with them and share their experiences.

Reach M. L. Pilgrim in mlpilgrim.author@gmail.com. Cheers!

Or subscribe to his newsletter for latest updates on his investment books.

BOOKS BY THIS AUTHOR

Best Ways to Invest in Gold For Beginners: Quick Guide for Learning and Investing in Gold. (BONUS: 14 Ways to Establish Real Gold from Fake Gold and more!)

Gold has kept a great value for thousands of years, and until this day it still occupies this high position, due to its properties that make it at the forefront of precious metals.

As it still retains its value throughout the ages, and the belief that is embedded in people's minds is that gold is the only way to pass and conserve wealth from one generation to another.

In times of political and economic tension as well as natural disasters, investors resort to buying gold as a safe haven in the markets and as a store of value, and it is also used as a hedge against high inflation. If you want gold to be part of your investment portfolio, you can choose from several investment options in gold, each of which has different investment characteristics. In this book, we offer many ways to invest in gold, tips to make the greatest possible start and the guide by which you can avoid fraud. We hope that we could help you, best of luck!

How to Understand The Subconscious Mind: Unlock, Unleash, and Let it Transform You!

What do you know about the subconscious mind?

Do you want to know more about its characteristics? It is within us, but it is elusive in many aspects. So, careful understanding of the subconscious mind will bring us many benefits.

This book will share about the ff:

- What is the subconscious mind?
- Its relationship with the conscious mind
- Methods of connecting with the subconscious mind
- Secrets of the subconscious mind
- The rules of the subconscious mind
- Using your subconscious mind to achieve your goals
- Programming the subconscious mind
- How to achieve sleep miracles
- Controlling your subconscious mind

So, what are you waiting for? Check out this informative yet insightful book in unleashing this mysterious power within ourselves.

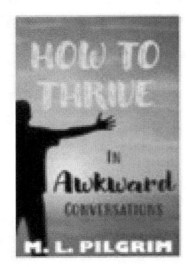 

How to Thrive in Awkward Conversations: Learn the Art of Speaking with Skill and Consideration (BONUS! 10 TIPS TO IMPROVE YOUR CONVERSATION SKILLS!)

Have you ever found yourself in the middle of an Awkward Conversation?

Conversation is an art of dealing and communicating with others. Effective Communication aims to build understanding and acceptance - not conflict. However, there is that other type of conversation - *the awkward conversation.*

When you are in the midst of an embarrassing moment, you see yourself in a situation you wished you were not. Hence, knowing what to do exactly in those moments will prepare you for the worst.

This book will help you on the ff:
- Importance of Speaking Tactfully
- What makes conversations awkward and how to avoid them?
- How to have perfect conversation with your partner?
- How to handle a conversation with your parents?
- Business and work conversations
- General Tips and Tricks to be a top speaker

Grab a copy of this book and start your journey into more assertive, confident, and tactful!

How to Say No to Yourself: Conquering Intermittent Fasting 101-The #1 Complete Guide for Beginners & Busy People (Bonus: No-Stress 30-Day Simple Plan, Meal Preparations, Cookbook and more!)

Intermittent fasting is currently one of the most popular health and fitness trends in the world. It will teach you the unique process of following alternative fasting and feeding cycles.

This book contains proven steps and strategies on how to intermittently fast for weight loss and also examines the concept of clean nutrition.

By reading it, you will learn practical and proven arts and practices that, if followed religiously, will create a young, vibrant, exuberant, radiant and totally different being.

Do you have to lose weight? Are you trying to adapt to that new outfit for the summer? But you don't want to fall in love with those diets and lose weight with the quick tricks of the past, you need something that really stands the test of time. Much more than a diet, you need a change in lifestyle. This is exactly what the 30-day intermittent fasting challenge offers. Intermittent fasting can restart and restore the body, helping to put metabolic processes back on track. Fasting teaches your body to burn fat instead of complex carbohydrates.

With your body poised and ready to burn fat for fuel, stubborn fatty deposits like your belly, arms and legs will evaporate quickly! It may sound too good to be true, but only by regulating the body through a dedicated and consistent fasting regimen - this is truly possible! This book provides you with the knowledge, background, and recipes to successfully perform your intermittent fasting regime over the course of 30 days.

In this book you will get:
Why fast?
What is intermittent fasting?
Intermittent fasting and your hormones
Intermittent fasting and weight loss
Eat Healthily
The Keto diet
Autophagy and intermittent fasting
Pagan's diet
Intermittent fasting methods
Intermediate fasting benefits
Dangers of intermittent fasting
Intermittent fasting programs

And, in essence, everything you need to learn how to apply the practice of intermittent fasting to your life program to reap immense intrinsic benefits and thus become a healthier, happier, better and, yes, richer being.

The Adventures of Sephas (Simple Bedtime Stories for Kids: Quick Read and Illustrations Included): The Boy who Speaks 100 Languages and Helps Many People All over the World

It is his 7th birthday, he got a gift. Little did he know what this gift can do for him ... Where will he go? What can he do? Can Sephas save the day?

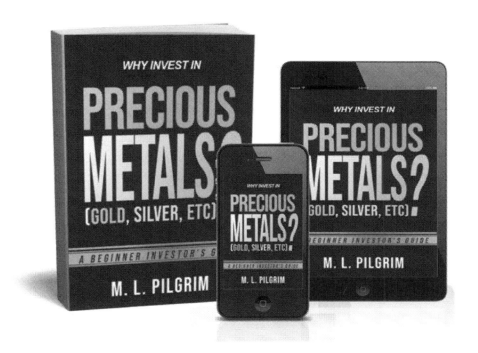

Don't Forget to <u>Claim</u> your FREE ebook!

OTHER PROMOTED BOOKS

S. K. PILGRIM

KENOSIS BOOKS: BE THE BEST YOU – SELF-IMPROVEMENT SERIES

SUBSCRIBE AND GET YOUR FREE eBOOK!

If you want to improve the quality of your attention and are willing to do other means to improve your focus and concentration, then this book will definitely help you in that. This book contains the ff:

1. Top Foods to increase your Focus and Concentration

2. Foods you can intake daily to improve your focus

3. Best Juices to Improve your focus

4. Healthy Habits and Eating Style to Improve Focus

..... and much more!

So take action, and scan the QR CODE and/or <u>Subscribe</u> *to our* **Kenosis Books - Be The Best You: Self-Improvement Series** *mailing list and be updated in our latest books and promotions!*

ABOUT THE AUTHOR

S.K. Pilgrim loves nature, travelling, food, and learning. He is a sport buff and loves running a lot. As a marathoner, he believes that keeping himself in good shape not only improves his running but also other aspects of his life. He loves reading books as well as writing them.

S.K. Pilgrim has a full-time job as senior leader in a multinational company. He is very passionate in coaching, training, and organizational development. He never gives up on any talent until they progress and improve to their potential!

Reach SK Pilgrim and our other authors in <u>kenosisbooks@gmail.com</u> Cheers!

BOOKS BY THIS AUTHOR

GIGA-ENERGY: High Energy Food - Turn-away from Sweets and Energy Drinks BONUS: Low Cholesterol and Low Sugar Energy Boosters

LOW ON ENERGY? HOW LONG CAN YOU SUSTAIN YOUR ENERGY?

Daily tasks and labor require a lot of energy but ending up on the vicious cycle of coffee, sweets, and high-energy drinks is detrimental to our health.

This book aims to share with you alternative sources of energy that will make you more energetic and last longer through more sustainable and healthy means.

- Instant Energy Boosters
- Long-term Energy Boosters
- Plant-Based Energy Boosters
- Juices and Smoothies Energy Boosters
- Daily Routines to Maintain Energy Levels
- Faster Metabolism and Weight Loss

- Energy-packed Breakfast
- and Much Much More!
- BONUS
  - Low-cholesterol Energy Boosters
  - Low-sugar Energy Boosters

Grab a copy of this book and let it lead you to GIGA-ENERGY lifestyle!

Don't Forget to <u>Claim</u> your FREE ebook!

Printed in Great Britain
by Amazon